THE
GLOUCESTERSHIRE WARWICKSHIRE RAILWAY

·A PAST AND PRESENT COMPANION·

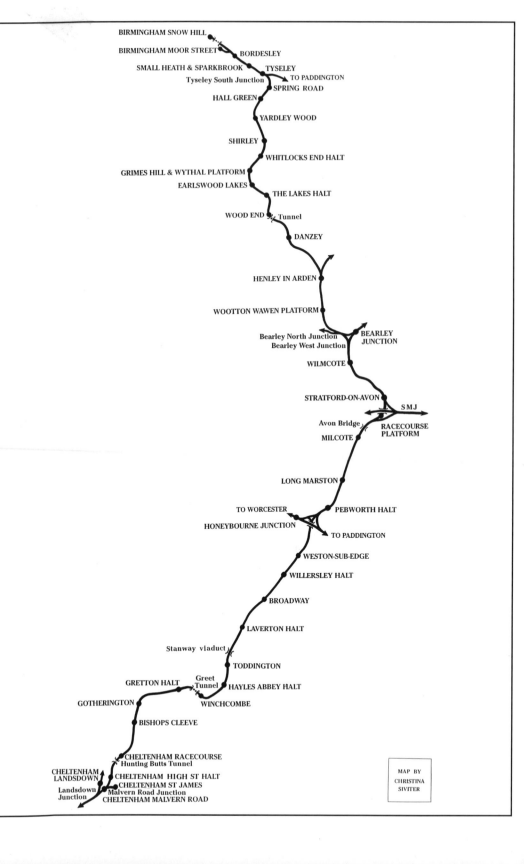

BIRMINGHAM SNOW HILL
BIRMINGHAM MOOR STREET
BORDESLEY
SMALL HEATH & SPARKBROOK
TYSELEY
Tyseley South Junction
TO PADDINGTON
SPRING ROAD
HALL GREEN
YARDLEY WOOD
SHIRLEY
WHITLOCKS END HALT
GRIMES HILL & WYTHAL PLATFORM
EARLSWOOD LAKES
THE LAKES HALT
WOOD END
Tunnel
DANZEY
HENLEY IN ARDEN
WOOTTON WAWEN PLATFORM
Bearley North Junction
Bearley West Junction
BEARLEY JUNCTION
WILMCOTE
STRATFORD-ON-AVON
SMJ
Avon Bridge
RACECOURSE PLATFORM
MILCOTE
LONG MARSTON
TO WORCESTER
PEBWORTH HALT
HONEYBOURNE JUNCTION
TO PADDINGTON
WESTON-SUB-EDGE
WILLERSLEY HALT
BROADWAY
LAVERTON HALT
Stanway viaduct
TODDINGTON
GRETTON HALT
Greet Tunnel
HAYLES ABBEY HALT
GOTHERINGTON
WINCHCOMBE
BISHOPS CLEEVE
CHELTENHAM RACECOURSE
Hunting Butts Tunnel
CHELTENHAM LANDSDOWN
CHELTENHAM HIGH ST HALT
CHELTENHAM ST JAMES
Landsdown Junction
Malvern Road Junction
CHELTENHAM MALVERN ROAD

MAP BY
CHRISTINA
SIVITER

THE
GLOUCESTERSHIRE
WARWICKSHIRE
RAILWAY

· A PAST and PRESENT COMPANION ·

A nostalgic trip along the whole route from Birmingham Snow Hill to Cheltenham

Roger Siviter ARPS

· RAILWAY HERITAGE ·
from
The NOSTALGIA Collection

First published as *British Railways Past and Present Special: Snow Hill to Cheltenham* in 1997
Reprinted 1999
New edition 2003

British Library Cataloguing in Publication Data

A catalogue record for this book is available from the British Library.

ISBN 1 85895 208 5

Past & Present Publishing Ltd
The Trundle
Ringstead Road
Great Addington
Kettering
Northants
NN14 4BW

Tel/Fax: 01536 330588
email: sales@nostalgiacollection.com
Website: www.nostalgiacollection.com

Maps drawn by Christina Siviter

The luggage labels, tickets and other items of ephemera were supplied by Winchcombe Railway Museum, 23 Gloucester Street, Winchcombe, Glos GL54 5HA.

Printed and bound in Great Britain

Past and
Present

A Past & Present book
from
The **NOSTALGIA** *Collection*

ACKNOWLEDGEMENTS

In compiling this book, I have been helped greatly by many people, and would like to take this opportunity to thank the following: Tyseley Museum; the management and staff of the Gloucestershire Warwickshire Railway, particularly Mr Collins and Mr Dudfield; The Stratford-on-Avon & Broadway Railway Society, in particular Audie Baker, whose knowledge and help have been invaluable; my wife Christina; Will Adams and Past & Present Publishing; Lens of Sutton; all the photographers accredited herein; and last but not least, all the railwaymen who make it all possible

BIBLIOGRAPHY

Baker, Audie *An Illustrated History of the Stratford-on-Avon to Cheltenham Railway* (Irwell Press)
Boynton, John *Shakespeare's Railways - The Lines Around Stratford-on-Avon Then and Now* (Mid England Books)
Christiansen, Rex *A Regional History of the Railways of Great Britain - Volume 7, The West Midlands* (David & Charles)
Harrison, Derek *Birmingham Snow Hill - A First Class Return* (Peter Watts Publishing)
Pigram, Ron & Edwards, Dennis F. *Cotswold Memories* (Unicorn Books)
Sleepers Awake, Volumes 1 and 2 (Gloucestershire Warwickshire Railway)
Whitehouse, John & Dowling, Geoff *British Railways Past and Present, No 5, The West Midlands* (Past and Present Publishing Ltd)
Railway World
Railway Magazine
Trains Illustrated

CONTENTS

On 12 August 1966 grimy Class '5' 4-6-0 No 44661 (shedded at Tyseley) climbs the 1 in 47 bank from Hockley into Birmingham Snow Hill station with a southbound mixed freight. Although the GWR route from Birmingham to Cheltenham opened in 1908, the new terminus at Moor Street did not open until July 1909, so for the first 12 months after the opening of the Cheltenham line, Snow Hill station was the Birmingham starting point for the route. *Roger Siviter*

INTRODUCTION

The former GWR route from Birmingham Snow Hill to Cheltenham Malvern Road station is often referred to as two separate sections, the first being the 25 miles from Birmingham to Stratford-on-Avon, otherwise known as the North Warwickshire Line. The terminus for this was Moor Street station, but Snow Hill was often the starting point for through trains from Birmingham, and further afield, to Cheltenham, Bristol and the West Country, with its attractive seaside resorts.

The second section of the route, from Stratford to Cheltenham Malvern Road, was 29 miles in length. Half a mile or so past Malvern Road station the line joined the main LMS route from Birmingham New Street to Gloucester and Bristol, thus giving the GWR a through route from Birmingham to the West Country.

The complete route from Birmingham to Cheltenham was opened in 1908, and on 1 July of that year the GWR inaugurated two express trains each way. One was the Wolverhampton to Penzance express, southbound in the morning and northbound in the evening; this was later to become the 'Cornishman'. The other train was from Cardiff to Norwich and Great Yarmouth via Leamington and Rugby, eastbound in the morning and westbound in the evening; however, this service did not last long. Originally all trains ran from Snow Hill, but on 1 July 1909 the GWR opened the new terminal at Moor Street, which greatly relieved the congestion at Snow Hill.

Today the North Warwickshire Line from Snow Hill to Stratford is still a busy commuter route, and although the old terminus at Moor Street is closed, it has, like Snow Hill, been rebuilt, but this time as a through station adjacent to its old namesake. The section of the line from Stratford to Cheltenham, after being under threat of closure since the late 1960s, and following a derailment at Winchcombe on 25 August 1975 that badly damaged the track, finally closed in 1976. The only section to remain open was from Honeybourne to Long Marston to serve the MOD depot and scrapyard. However, this was not the end because, thanks to four individuals, the Gloucestershire Warwickshire Railway was formed in 1981, and by 1987 trains were running between the headquarters of the 'new' railway at Toddington and Winchcombe. The ultimate aim is that one day the line may run from Stratford to the outskirts of Cheltenham.

There is also the Stratford-on-Avon & Broadway Railway Society, formed in July 1995, which has an operating base within the MOD depot at Long Marston. The society was formed to promote the reinstatement of the 15 miles between Stratford and Broadway.

In its heyday in the 1930s the route was fairly busy, with many local trains from Birmingham to Cheltenham being worked by GWR diesel railcars. The decline set in after the war, although the Wolverhampton to Penzance working was restored, and in 1952 was named the 'Cornishman'.

In its last few years the line was used mainly as a freight route, with much traffic from South Wales to the Midlands and further afield; indeed the 1975 derailment at Winchcombe, which hastened the line's demise, was of a freight train to Severn Tunnel Junction.

The route of the line gives the passenger many contrasts. After leaving the industrial area south-east of Birmingham at Tyseley South junction (where it diverges from the main line to Paddington), it runs through the pleasant suburbs of Hall Green, Yardley and Shirley, then through the attractive North Warwickshire countryside to the Shakespearean town of Stratford-on-Avon, via such places as Earlswood and Henley-on-Arden.

A few miles after running through the Warwickshire countryside south of Stratford, and passing under the Worcester to Paddington line at Honeybourne, the line skirts the edge of the Cotswolds, calling at the famous old Worcestershire town of Broadway. A mile or so further on the route enters Gloucestershire, calling at many picturesque Cotswold villages before arriving in the world-famous Regency town of Cheltenham Spa, some 54 miles from Birmingham.

The main locomotive depot for the route was at Tyseley, coded 84E in Western Region days, then 2A in 1963, when regional boundary changes saw the London Midland Region take over the area. The steam shed was closed in 1966, but through the efforts of many people, led by the late Patrick Whitehouse, and with the backing of the City of Birmingham, part of the depot became a working museum, although the actual steam shed was demolished in 1969. It has many famous residents, including 'Castle' Class 4-6-0 No 7029 *Clun Castle* and 'Jubilee' Class 4-6-0 No 5593 *Kolhapur*, locomotives that regularly run on the main line and, as we shall see later, on many trips to Stratford-on-Avon and back. A Traction Maintenance Depot, situated nearer to the main line, provides servicing facilities, etc, for the many DMUs at work in the West Midlands. There were also small sheds at Stratford and Cheltenham Malvern Road, the former closing in 1962, and the latter in 1964.

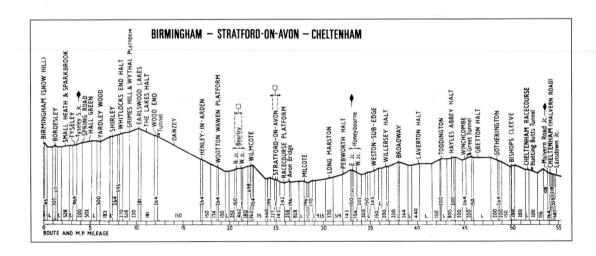

BIRMINGHAM TO STRATFORD-ON-AVON

Snow Hill

Ex-GWR 'Grange' Class 4-6-0 No 6861 *Crynant Grange* pulls into Snow Hill with a Saturdays-only holiday train from Wolverhampton to the Southern Region in August 1961. A green-liveried diesel multiple unit (DMU) is seen in the bay platform on the right-hand side of the picture, probably forming a local service to Worcester via Kidderminster.

Snow Hill station consisted of two island platforms, each some 1,200 feet in length; their northern ends each contained two bay platforms. Because the main platforms could accommodate two trains at once, they were given two separate platform numbers, which, together with the bays, made a total of 12 platforms. In the late 1940s, on summer Saturdays when I was busy 'trainspotting' at Snow Hill, it was not uncommon for there to be a train at each main platform, plus more waiting to enter the station.

On 16 January 1997 Class 150 unit No 150017 pulls into the 'new' Snow Hill station with the 1258 Stourbridge Junction-Stratford-on-Avon service. The station closed in 1972, but was rebuilt and opened again in 1987, thanks to the efforts of the local transport authority. A contributing factor to this must have been that, due to a closure agreement, the trackbed remained intact. A comparison between the two pictures shows the trackbed to be the same, but the new platforms are shorter and there are now only two tracks between them. Some of the buildings in the background remain the same, but there are some new additions, notably the blocks of flats on the right-hand side. *Norman Preedy/RS*

Turning round from the previous picture, we see Class '5' 4-6-0 Nos 44477 and 45352 heading north through Snow Hill on 12 August 1966. This view (looking towards Paddington) gives some idea of the length and spaciousness of the main platforms, and also shows the splendid roof. The original Snow Hill station was built in 1852, but due to the increase in rail traffic was rebuilt in 1871, and again in 1910 in the form that we see here.

At the rear of the locomotives can be seen some of the bridge girders that carried the station over Great Charles Street, where there was an entrance to the station. Also, above the rear of the second locomotive can just be seen one of the station's two large clocks. Also dominating the scene is a huge office block belonging to Stewarts & Lloyds Steel Company.

On 16 January 1997 the office block (now West Midlands Police HQ) is still there, but the new Snow Hill bears very little resemblance to the previous station. The roof is now a car park, and instead of 12 platforms there are now just three, with a fourth numbered but as yet without any track. Note also the bridge girders (to the left of the train) where the station crosses over the new expressway (formerly Great Charles Street). The 165 'Turbo' unit is forming the 1330 service to London Marylebone. These trains are a fairly new addition to the timetable and provide a very useful alternative service to London, running at hourly intervals throughout the day. Although the new Snow Hill can never take the place of its illustrious predecessor, it is nice to see a station reborn again, and thus keeping something of the old GWR alive in the Birmingham area. *Both RS*

On the morning of Saturday 30 April 1966 'Black Five' 4-6-0 No 44872 pauses at Snow Hill with a Ffestiniog Railway special from Paddington to Portmadoc. The sign for the Great Charles Street entrance can be seen clearly on the left-hand side of the picture. The station had three entrances, the others being the main one on the corner of Livery Street and Colmore Row, and a further side entrance in Snow Hill itself.

On 16 January 1997 Class 150 No 150126 stands at the new platform 2 with the 1405 service to Shirley. This picture was taken at roughly the same spot as the previous scene and provides a tremendous and obvious contrast. *Both RS*

Ex-GWR 0-6-0 pannier tank Nos 9630 and 9610 emerge from Snow Hill Tunnel and enter Snow Hill station from the Paddington direction on Sunday 11 September 1966 with the stock of a special train organised by the Stephenson Locomotive Society, billed as a 'Farewell to the GWR 0-6-0 Pannier Tanks'. The train's itinerary, starting from Snow Hill, was Old Hill, Halesowen, Old Hill, Dudley, Wolverhampton Low Level, Birmingham Snow Hill, Henley-in-Arden, Stratford-on-Avon, Leamington Spa and back to Snow Hill. This view again gives some idea of the size of the station's magnificent roof and shows how spacious the platforms were, together with some of the many amenities that were available to the passengers.

This view of Snow Hill on 16 January 1997 makes it look like an underground station, and only the entrance to Snow Hill tunnel bears comparison with the previous scene. The train is the rear of the 1405 service to Shirley with 150 unit No 150126. *Both RS*

'Hall' Class 4-6-0 No 6935 *Browsholme Hall* is seen at Snow Hill's outer platform No 12 on 16 April 1960, in charge of the 5.45 pm to Stratford-on-Avon and Worcester. Note the smoke trough above the locomotive.

Before leaving Snow Hill, mention must be made of the two large and handsome clocks, one on platform 7 (see the picture on page 10) and the other outside the booking hall. I am sure that this latter clock in particular will bring back fond memories of the old Snow Hill station to many generations of people from Birmingham and further afield, who met their friends and relations 'under the clock'; I can certainly vouch for this personally.

For outer platform No 12, now read outer platform No 4, as this view taken at Snow Hill on 16 January 1997 shows. As yet the track is waiting to be laid, but the curvature of the platform edge is almost the same as in the previous scene. *Michael Mensing/RS*

Moor Street

On 2 July 1960 ex-GWR 'Hall' Class 4-6-0 No 5996 *Mytton Hall* (shedded at Worcester, 85A) pulls out of Snow Hill tunnel with the 5.45 pm Birmingham Snow Hill to Stratford-on-Avon and Worcester train and passes by the side of Moor Street station. The bridge girders seen under the second coach carry the line over the LMR lines into New Street station from Euston and the North and East of England. In the left background can be seen the edge of the rear of the large Marks & Spencer store.

On 16 January 1997 'Turbo' unit No 165006 calls at the new Moor Street station with the 1230 Snow Hill to Marylebone service; the girders of the bridge over the LMR route can be seen by the second coach, and the Marks & Spencer building is still prominent. At the back of the train can be seen the entrance to Snow Hill tunnel. In September 1987, just before the new Moor Street and Snow Hill stations opened, the public was invited to walk through the newly refurbished tunnel, and 14,000 people turned up to do so. *Michael Mensing/RS*

On the morning of 10 June 1973 LNER Class 'V2' 2-6-2 No 4771 *Green Arrow* backs into Moor Street station in order to take out a special train to Stratford-on-Avon. This was the first of three return trains that were run that day to Shakespeare's home town. This scene, taken with a telephoto lens from Moor Street itself, shows clearly the trackbed of the lines to Snow Hill station, which were taken up shortly after closure of the station in 1972. In the distance the track can be seen curving away across Bordesley viaduct (797 yards long) towards Bordesley station, Small Heath and Tyseley (junction for the North Warwickshire Line).

Today's wider view, again taken on 16 January 1997, shows the new Moor Street from the northern side. On the right-hand side, just above one of the new station's shelters, can be seen one of the platform canopies of the old station. A modern signal gantry now controls movements at the new station's platform ends. Because the modern-looking building on the left-hand side has disappeared, more of Bordesley viaduct can be seen. The foreground building with the round corrugated iron roof seems to have stood the test of time. *Both RS*

This photograph, taken from the front entrance, shows the old Moor Street station on 13 November 1985. On the right-hand side is the empty stock of the 1210 Stratford-on-Avon train, while waiting at platform 3 is the 1140 service to Shirley. This station was closed shortly after the new one was opened in September 1987, with the hope that one day it would become a museum. However, the present view, taken on 16 January 1997, shows that this might still be some way off, although the comparison shows that happily much remains intact. *Both RS*

On 28 July 1960 ex-GWR '5600' Class 0-6-2 tank No 6668, having brought in the 6.25 pm from Knowle & Dorridge, is seen moving off one of the two locomotive traversers that were sited at the terminus end of Moor Street station. The fine-looking goods shed dominates the background.

Because the station is now fenced on three sides as a necessary deterrent against vandalism, it was only possible to photograph the present scene from an approximately similar angle. This picture, taken through the bars guarding the main entrance, shows that where the goods shed was situated is now a car park and, although the tracks are still there, the traversers disappeared long ago. The present scene also shows some of the very pleasant station architecture, typical of the GWR in its heyday. *Michael Mensing/RS*

19

This final 'past' scene, taken at Moor Street on a very sunny 13 November 1985, shows well the three platforms and splendid canopies, as well as the attractive roof of the booking hall, etc. The DMU in the siding will, after the departure of the 1140 to Shirley (out of sight behind it) move out and reverse back into platform 3 to form the 1210 to Stratford-on-Avon, for which there are already people waiting in the November sunshine.

These pictures were taken from the edge of the car park where the goods shed once stood. Apart from the weeds, the station was very much intact and complete with nameboard on 16 January 1997; beyond can be seen one side of the new station. The main change is in the background. Marks & Spencer is still there, but the other stores have been obscured by the new 'Pavilions' shopping centre. Also, the balloon has disappeared! *Both RS*

Bordesley and Small Heath

The first station on the line from Snow Hill/Moor Street was, and still is, Bordesley, which opened in 1855. This 'past' picture, looking westwards in the mid-1960s, shows a neat GWR suburban station through which ran four tracks - two main and two relief. The station also boasted cattle docks and sidings to service the nearby markets. In the distance can be seen an abundance of semaphore signals and a signal box.

Today the station is but a shadow of itself. Only the down platform remains, with a small 'bus shelter'. The remains of the up platform (from which the previous picture was taken) can still be seen, and the building on the right-hand side provides a link between the two views, as does the metal fence on the left-hand side. Three tracks now run through the station, but the sidings have long since gone. *Lens of Sutton/RS*

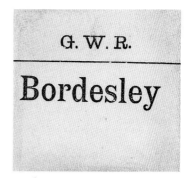

G. W. R.

Bordesley

On 20 July 1961 GWR '5100' Class 2-6-2 tank No 5174 is seen crossing from the relief to the main lines at Bordesley station with the 6.25 pm from Knowle & Dorridge to Moor Street. In the background can be seen the LMR Camp Hill relief line from Landor Street junction near Saltley on the Derby line, to Kings Norton on the line to Bristol. This relief line is used mainly by freight trains, but also acts as a New Street station avoiding line.

In 1961 Bordesley was a fairly busy station, especially on Saturday afternoons when the 'Blues' (Birmingham City Football Club) were at home at their nearby ground at St Andrew's. Nowadays only a couple of trains (morning and evening) stop here, for the convenience of the local factory workers, although one or two trains still stop here when the 'Blues' are at home. The 'present' picture, taken on 5 October 1996, shows the rear of a midday Snow Hill to Shirley train, comprising Class 150 unit No 150122. The Camp Hill relief line can still be seen, but the sidings have disappeared as well as the bracket signals. A new rail bridge has also been installed where the tracks cross over the expressway. *Michael Mensing/RS*

A mile or so west of Bordesley station, our line approaches Small Heath & Sparkbrook station. The first view, taken on 21 July 1962, shows a three-car WR suburban DMU on the 1.10 pm Birmingham Moor Street to Henley-in-Arden service approaching the station; it also shows the busy goods yard and sidings situated to the north of the main line. Note the water tower standing at the top of the embankment.

The second picture, taken with a telephoto lens on 9 October 1982, shows that the goods yard has disappeared, but gives a view of the car-carrier sidings (extreme left) situated to the south of the main line. Beyond the girder bridge, near to the site of the old goods yard, is Bordesley Junction, where one line swings northwards to connect with the LMS Camp Hill relief line, providing a through route from the Paddington-Birmingham line to the Birmingham-Derby/Leicester lines, which over the years has been used by many steam specials. This special, hauled by GWR 'Castle' Class 4-6-0 No 5051 *Earl Bathurst*, is a return working to Didcot from Moor Street, the outward journey having called at Stratford-on-Avon via Hatton and Bearley Junction, then on to Birmingham via the North Warwickshire Line.

The final photograph in this sequence is a composite view of the previous two, taken on 5 October 1996, and shows Class 150 unit No 150130 with the 1015 Stourbridge Junction-Snow Hill-Shirley service. As in the previous pictures, the trackwork remains basically the same, and more can be seen of the car-carrier sidings, but a comparison with the 1962 scene shows that the signal box, hut, water tower and some trackwork have long since disappeared. Tower blocks and high-rise city buildings have been built, including the Rotunda and the Post Office Tower, while the older houses have been demolished.
Michael Mensing/RS (2)

Small Heath & Sparkbrook station was opened in 1863 and this view, looking westwards in the mid-1960s, shows well the two spacious island platforms, complete with waiting rooms and fine canopy roofs. The main station offices and booking hall can just be seen behind the canopy on the left-hand side. Also on this side, under the bridge, can be glimpsed the car-carrier sidings. The four main tracks that ran through the station continued on to Lapworth on the main Paddington route, and were necessary to cope with the heavy suburban traffic between Birmingham and the Solihull area.

The scene at the station on Saturday 25 January 1997 shows that the GWR booking hall is still there and in use, but the platform buildings have gone, to be replaced by one small 'bus shelter'. Both up and down trains now use only the down platform, although the up platform still looks intact. The houses at the top of the 'past' picture have obviously gone, but there are still four main tracks through the station, as well as the sidings, etc, on the left-hand side. *Lens of Sutton/RS*

Tyseley

On 15 May 1966, when the shed was in the London Midland Region and numbered 2A, BR Standard Class '9F' 2-10-0 No 92002 stands alongside '8F' 2-8-0 No 48861. In its heyday in the 1950s, Tyseley shed had an allocation of around 100 locomotives, including 'Hall' and 'Grange' Class 4-6-0s, but by the 1960s this had reduced to 50-60 locomotives. The shed closed at the end of 1966, but happily it became a working museum. This 'present' photograph was taken on 8 January 1997 roughly from where the previous one was taken. The actual shed building has gone (hopefully to be rebuilt one day) and only one of the two 65-foot turntables that it housed now remains. On the right-hand side of the picture can be seen the large repair workshop where work is carried out on the museum's own locomotives, as well as engines from far and wide. At the back of the repair shop can just be seen the coaling plant, and at the back of coach No 7 can be seen the shed office. The museum is open all the year round, and among its attractions are courses on locomotive driving. *Both RS*

Above In around 1957 (when the shed was still in the Western Region and numbered 84E) an illustrious visitor was GWR 4-4-0 No 3440 *City of Truro*. This locomotive, designed by Churchward and introduced in 1903, was withdrawn in 1931 but returned to service in 1957 to work special trains. *Author's collection*

Below On Sunday 15 May 1966 the only ex-GWR-type tender locomotive (apart from those preserved) still working on BR was 'Castle' Class 4-6-0 No 7029, formerly *Clun Castle*, seen here being serviced at Tyseley shed, its home base. At that time it would sometimes work an early evening van train to and from Banbury. *RS*

By the side of Tyseley shed (situated adjacent to the Warwick Road and very convenient for loco spotting!) was the shed yard where, on 9 October 1965, BR Standard Class '5MT' 4-6-0 No 73026 poses in front of a 'Black Five' 4-6-0, behind which can be seen part of the shed building.

The same scene on 8 January 1997 shows that the old shed yard is used mainly as a car park for the museum, which can be seen clearly at the back of the yard. The carriage sidings on the right are situated next to the main line. *Both RS*

Just to the west of Tyseley shed is Tyseley station where, on 30 August 1958, Standard Class '5' 4-6-0 No 73014 is seen in charge of the 8.30 am Pembroke Dock to Birmingham Snow Hill train. The station is very similar to Small Heath, with its two island platforms straddled by the station offices, but unlike Small Heath, which was opened in 1863, it was not opened until 1906.

On 8 January 1997 we see the rear of Class 150 unit No 150104 departing for Leamington Spa with the 1157 from Worcester Foregate Street. As can be seen, Tyseley station today is in very good order, and still with its station buildings and canopies (although minus a couple of chimneys). A comparison with the earlier picture shows that the signal box (beyond the bridge at the rear of the train), which controlled the junction to the North Warwickshire Line, has gone, but the buildings and hoardings on the left are largely unchanged. It seems appropriate that this attractive facility is the station for the Birmingham Railway Museum. *Michael Mensing/RS*

G. W. R.

Tyseley

These next four scenes, taken over the last 31 years, show the south side of Tyseley station looking towards Snow Hill, with the entrance to the carriage sidings and locomotive shed on the left. The running lines are used mainly but not exclusively by traffic for the North Warwickshire Line.

The first picture, taken on 1 February 1966, shows ex-LMS Class 2MT 2-6-0 No 46457 heading for the North Warwickshire Line with a load of coal wagons. At this time semaphore signals were very much in evidence. To the left of the train can be seen the lines leading to the sidings and shed.

When steam finished on BR in August 1968, for the next three years (apart from trips by No 4472 *Flying Scotsman*) there was a complete ban on steam workings on the main line. Therefore preserved lines and steam centres such as Tyseley came into their own, providing not only the enthusiast but the general public with the taste of steam. The Birmingham Railway Museum, with its own locomotives, was able to stage 'open days' complete with short 'trip' workings behind steam. One of the first of these, if not indeed the very first, was on Sunday 29 September 1968, arranged by Patrick Whitehouse of the museum and British Railways. A short shuttle service was run from near the old shed to the junction for the North Warwickshire Line, with GWR 'Castle' Class 4-6-0 No 7029 at one end and LMS 'Jubilee' Class 4-6-0 No 5593 *Kholapur* at the other. Here we see *Kholapur* propelling the shuttle service past Tyseley station. A comparison with the previous picture shows that

some of the trackwork has been taken up and some of the semaphores have already gone. The shed building, which can be seen on the left-hand side, was demolished in the following year.

This scene was repeated on 3 June 1973 when the illustrious visitor LNER 'A4' 'Pacific' No 4498 *Sir Nigel Gresley* headed towards the museum area with the shuttle service; at the rear of the train was another LNER stalwart, Class 'V2' 2-6-2 No 4771 *Green Arrow*. Steam had by now resumed on BR and both locomotives were at Tyseley to work steam specials in the area, with No 4771 working a series of return trips to Stratford-on-Avon on the following weekend. A little later (1 July 1973) both engines would work return specials to the GWR depot at Didcot. Compared with the previous picture, the trackwork and station look the same, but the semaphores now have gone completely. As stated before, the shed building had gone by now, but most of the other railway buildings are still there, and a new-looking factory has appeared on the left-hand sky-line.

The final scene was taken on 8 January 1997 and shows the rear of Class 150 unit No 150127 as it enters the station with the 1239 service from Shirley to Snow Hill and Stourbridge Junction. Not a lot has changed since the previous picture, but the carriage shed, which was situated behind the brick hut on the left hand side, has disappeared, and a roadway and barrier have appeared in the foreground. Also both the new and the old factory buildings have now gone. *All RS*

BR Standard Class '9F' 2-10-0 No 92094 approaches Tyseley station with a goods train from the Banbury area on 1 February 1966. This is Tyseley South junction, and the North Warwickshire Line to Stratford can be seen coming in from the right.

On 29 September 1968 (*right*) No 7029 *Clun Castle* looks a treat as it works one end of the open day shuttle already seen on page 32, with *Kholapur* at the other end. By now some of the trackwork has gone, together with the appropriate semaphore signals, but the GWR signal box is still there.

The same scene today sees the 1239 from Shirley (Class 150 unit No 150127) approaching Tyseley station on 8 January 1997. The trackwork is the same as in 1968, but the box and signals have gone, as well as the church! The old terraced houses on the left survive, but the factory chimney has gone. *All RS*

North Warwickshire Line

The first station on the North Warwickshire Line is Spring Road Platform, which was opened 1n 1908. On 17 June 1959 (*above*) ex-GWR 'Modified Hall' Class 4-6-0 No 6982 *Melmerby Hall* heads through Spring Road with a southbound coal train.

At the same spot today (*above right*) all that can be seen is a short section of the line emerging from beneath a two-storey car park, which serves the adjacent Lucas factory. Beyond the car park, the third view shows Spring Road station today, with Class 150 unit No 150120 about to depart with the 1327 Stratford to Stourbridge Junction service. A comparison with the 1959 view shows that the platform buildings have been replaced with a modern 'bus shelter' and lighting, but the building to the left of the bridge is still there, as is the factory building seen above the road bridge. The semaphore signals disappeared long ago, but as yet only the northbound track has concrete sleepers. Both 'present' pictures were taken on 8 January 1997. *Michael Mensing/RS (2)*

On the morning of Sunday 10 June 1973 ex-LNER Class 'V2' 2-6-2 No 4771 *Green Arrow* races through Hall Green station with the first of three special trains run from Moor Street to Stratford and return by the LCGB in association with Birmingham Railway Museum.

Twenty-four years later, on 25 January 1997, Class 150 unit No 150127 starts away from the station after pausing with the 1412 Stourbridge Junction to Stratford service. Apart from the station nameboards very little has changed over the years - there is even a man in the same place on the northbound platform! If anything, this station, opened in 1908, looks in better shape today than it did in 1973. *Both RS*

Also opened in 1908 (as was Shirley, the next station down the line) was Yardley Wood where, on 8 August 1959, ex-GWR 'Hall' Class 4-6-0 No 5988 *Bostock Hall* is seen pulling through the station with the 2.45 pm Birmingham Snow Hill to Fishguard Harbour train. This locomotive and train had previously worked into Snow Hill with a train from Swansea, due in at 2.09 pm, thus necessitating a smart turn-round.

On 25 January 1997 Class 150 unit No 150104 pauses at Yardley Wood with the 1358 Stourbridge Junction to Stratford service. The modern lighting has replaced the old GWR-type lamps, and the GWR canopy has given way to a modern structure, as have the station nameboards. *Michael Mensing/RS*

On Saturday 29 August 1959 'Modified Hall' Class 4-6-0 No 6971 *Athelhampton Hall* passes through Shirley station with the 3.45 pm Snow Hill to Swansea train. Some 38 years later, on 25 January 1997, Class 150 unit No 150002 enters Shirley station, where it will terminate, with the 1405 from Snow Hill. Concrete sleepers have now replaced the wooden ones, but as can be seen the station buildings are in excellent condition, and workmen can be seen repairing the southbound platform roof. Sadly, the footbridge roof has gone, as have the old station lamps, but these have been replaced with fine-looking reproductions. Semaphore signals still control the station area, but these are now upper-quadrant. Shirley still boasts a handsome GWR signal box, which is out of sight at the back of the train, next to the southbound line. *Michael Mensing/RS*

Around a mile from Shirley is Whitlocks End Halt where, on 3 May 1969, a three-car Western suburban DMU pauses with the 4.10 pm Birmingham Moor Street to Stratford train. This halt was opened in 1936.

The same scene is enacted on 25 January 1997 as Class 150 unit No 150118 prepares to leave with the 1258 Stourbridge Junction to Stratford service. New 'bus shelters' have replaced the old buildings, and there are modern station nameboards and lighting. Also the road bridge at the back of the train has been replaced with one of concrete construction. The power lines and poles are still there, however. *Michael Mensing/RS*

On 14 April 1963 a three-car Western suburban set pauses at Grimes Hill & Wythall with the 10.35 am Stratford to Snow Hill train. On 6 February 1997 the same station, now known as just plain Wythall, plays host to Class 150 unit No 150017 as it arrives with the 1227 Stratford to Stourbridge Junction train. The station nameboard has obviously changed, and the small hut and cycle shed are long gone, but happily the GWR-type booking office remains in situ, and is still in use. 'Bus shelters' have replaced the platform waiting rooms. *Michael Mensing/RS*

'Castle' Class 4-6-0 No 5046 *Earl Cawdor* approaches Earlswood Lakes station with an excursion train from Birmingham Snow Hill to Weston-super-Mare on 31 May 1959. By contrast, on 25 January 1997 Class 150 unit No 150016 nears Earlswood station with the 1158 Stourbridge Junction to Stratford train. The loop line and the semaphore signals have gone, and the embankment is completely overgrown. Only the gable end of the house, glimpsed through the foliage above the unit, gives us a point of identification with the earlier picture. *Michael Mensing/RS*

45

Turning round from the previous pictures, we see ex-GWR 2-6-2 tank No 4170 preparing to leave Earlswood Lakes station with a Stratford to Birmingham train in April 1957. Today's scene shows unit No 150104 forming the 1227 Stratford to Stourbridge Junction service on 25 January 1997. Much has changed over the intervening 40 years; the station is now known as Earlswood (Earlswood West Midlands in the timetable) and all the platform buildings and water tower, etc, have disappeared. Despite the station's bareness, the platforms and fences seem to be in good order and, as can be seen, it is very well lit. This station, together with Grimes Hill & Wythall, was opened in 1908. *R. S. Carpenter collection/RS*

The Lakes Halt (some 11 miles from Snow Hill) was opened in 1935. On 26 May 1964 a three-car WR suburban DMU enters the halt with the 6.10 pm service from Moor Street to Henley-in-Arden. The 'present' equivalent was taken on 25 January 1997 and shows No 150104 entering The Lakes (as it is now known in the timetable) with the 1058 Stourbridge Junction to Stratford service. As elsewhere, modern 'bus shelters' have replaced the old waiting rooms, and the telegraph poles have gone, but once again there is good lighting on the platforms and a large timetable board. The houses in the background can still be glimpsed through the trees, and a variety of garden sheds and greenhouses have sprung up over the years. This small station is yet another example of the high standard of many of the stations on the North Warwickshire Line. *Michael Mensing/RS*

Wood End was opened in 1908, when it was known as Wood End Platform; like Spring Road, Yardley Wood, Grimes Hill and Wootton Wawen, this was the GWR's way of denoting a minor station, but the suffix had been dropped from them all by the 1970s.

Wood End Tunnel is immediately south of the station, and on 12 November 1966 'Britannia' 'Pacific' No 70004, formerly *William Shakespeare*, has just left the 175-yard-long curving tunnel and hurries through Wood End station with the LCGB 'Shakespeare Special' from Waterloo to Birmingham Snow Hill via Oxford, Banbury and Stratford-on-Avon, returning via High Wycombe and Kensington to Victoria. Note the SR stock.

On 8 June 1985 'Castle' Class 4-6-0 No 7029 *Clun Castle* climbs through Wood End with the 11.05 Stratford to Birmingham (Hall Green) special train. This was one of a series of special charters run that day by Birmingham Railway Museum. The embankment is becoming overgrown and the telegraph poles have gone, but the concrete footbridge is still there, providing access for passengers to the station. Once again there is a plentiful supply of modern lighting and the platform buildings have changed.

The final scene at Wood End was taken on 6 February 1997 and shows No 150103 leaving the station with the 1327 Stratford to Stourbridge Junction train. There has been very little further change over the last 12 years, the most notable being that concrete sleepers have replaced the old wooden ones. *All RS*

G. W. R.

Wood End

G. W. R.

DANZEY
(For TANWORTH)

The next location is Danzey for Tanworth station, which opened in 1908, looking north in July 1964. Northbound trains face a 10-mile climb of about 1 in 150 from just south of Wootton Wawen to Earlswood Lakes station.

On 25 January 1997 Danzey station still looks in reasonable order, complete with an old station nameboard that now reads only 'Danzey' rather than 'Danzey for Tanworth' as in the earlier picture. The signal box, points and sidings have all gone, but the shed by the main siding is still there and the old goods yard is now fenced off and used as a contractors' yard. The small waiting room has been replaced by a modern 'bus shelter' and the fencing is now painted white, but the flower borders have disappeared. This view shows that we are now in the heart of the very pleasant North Warwickshire countryside. *R. S. Carpenter collection/RS*

Some 3 miles south of Danzey is the ancient town of Henley-in-Arden, and this is a view of the fine-looking station taken around 1960, looking towards Birmingham.

In common with many of the places served by this route, Henley can still boast a neat and pleasant station, as the 'present' view taken on 25 January 1997 confirms. The only radical change is the disappearance of the northbound platform waiting room, replaced by a small shelter at the foot of the handsome station footbridge. Semaphore signals, now upper quadrant, are still in use and controlled by the GWR signal box, clearly seen under the footbridge. Note also the modern lighting.

Originally, Henley was served by a short branch from Rowington, just south of Lapworth on the Birmingham-Paddington line, the station for this line being to the north-east of the present one. When today's station was opened in 1908 it was connected to the branch, thus providing two routes to Birmingham, but the branch to Rowington was closed in 1917. The left-hand side of the island platform was used as the bay platform for the branch train, the earlier station having closed to passenger traffic in 1908. *Lens of Sutton/RS*

G.W.R.

Henley-in-Arden

Opposite page As mentioned above, when Wootton Wawen station opened in 1908 it was designated a 'Platform', a name that it retained until 1974 when it became plain Wootton Wawen (the last 'Platform' on the ex-GWR system to lose the suffix). In the 'past' view, taken in the early 1960s, the old name can be seen clearly, together with the station buildings from that period.

In today's view, taken on 6 February 1997, 'bus shelters' have replaced the previous building and the station is now equipped with modern lighting. The telegraph poles have gone, and the wooden sleepers have been replaced by concrete ones. *Lens of Sutton/RS*

This page Ex-GWR 'Modified Hall' Class 4-6-0 No 7919 *Runter Hall* is seen north of Bearley Junction with the 5.45 pm Snow Hill to Stratford train on 8 August 1964. Apart from the motive power very little appears to have changed in the 'present' picture, taken on 20 February 1997. The train is the 1258 from Stourbridge Junction to Stratford-on-Avon, formed by Class 150 unit No 150120. The main change is the growth of bushes and trees. *Michael Mensing/RS*

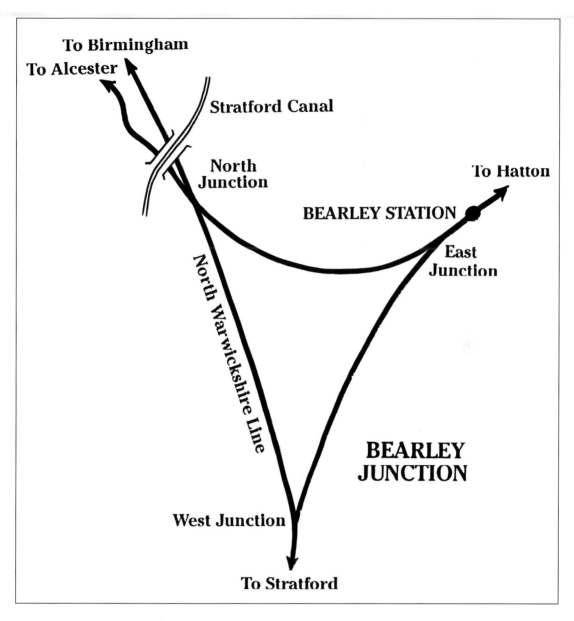

To Birmingham

To Alcester

Stratford Canal

North Junction

To Hatton

BEARLEY STATION

East Junction

North Warwickshire Line

BEARLEY JUNCTION

West Junction

To Stratford

Turning round from the previous view, first of all we see Brush Type 4 No D1914 on 6 August 1966 as it heads north out of Bearley Junction with the 10.00 am train from Plymouth to Birmingham. On 20 February 1997 Class 150 unit No 150120 heads north at the same location with the 1423 Stratford to Stourbridge Junction service. The platelayers' hut and telegraph poles have now gone and the trees have grown, but otherwise not a great deal has changed.

These and the previous two pictures were taken from Edstone aqueduct, which carries the Stratford-on-Avon Canal over the line, hence the reason for the widening of the gap between the tracks. Also at this point was the junction for the line to Alcester, which closed in 1951. This provided a connection from Hatton on the Birmingham-Paddington line via Bearley East and North junctions to Alcester, which was situated on the Redditch-Ashchurch route (known as the Gloucester loop line), but this former Midland line was closed in 1963. *Michael Mensing/RS*

G.W.R

BEARLEY

Opposite page About a mile south of Bearley Junction is the picturesque village of Wilmcote, famous as the home of Mary Arden, Shakespeare's mother. This view of the attractive station, which is separated from the village by the Stratford-on-Avon Canal, was taken looking towards Stratford in the early 1960s.

This station is very well preserved, as can be seen from the 'present' view taken on 6 February 1997. The only changes, as so often on this line, seem to be the lighting, station nameboards and modern concrete sleepers. *Lens of Sutton/RS*

This view of Wilmcote station, looking north, was taken on 8 December 1991, and shows a Metropolitan-Cammell Class 101 DMU No 51410 pausing at the station with a midday Leamington Spa to Stratford service, via Hatton and Bearley Junction. The unit is in GWR chocolate-and-cream livery, which fits in very well with this fine-looking station. *RS*

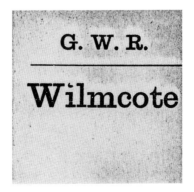

G. W. R.

Wilmcote

For the 2½ miles between Stratford-on-Avon and Wilmcote, northbound trains face a steep climb, mainly at 1 in 75, and on 15 June 1957 ex-GWR 'Castle' Class 4-6-0 No 5047 *Earl of Dartmouth* makes a fine sight as it approaches the summit of Wilmcote bank with the main portion of the 'Cornishman' from Penzance to Wolverhampton. Although this working was discontinued during the war years it was re-instated afterwards, and in the summer of 1952 received its name. The 'Cornishman' continued to run on the route until 7 September 1962, when it was diverted to the former Midland Lickey route. On summer Saturdays in the 1950s it would often run in several portions.

The 'present' scene shows Class 150 unit No 150105 climbing Wilmcote bank on 25 February 1997 with the 1327 Stratford to Stourbridge Junction service. The right-hand bank is now almost completely overgrown and only the curve at the back of the train and the bank on the left-hand side provide any identification with the earlier picture. *Michael Mensing/RS*

59

INTERLUDE: PRESERVED STEAM ON THE NORTH WARWICKSHIRE LINE

Since the early 1970s many special steam trips have been run on the North Warwickshire Line. Several steam weekends have also been organised by the Birmingham Railway Museum at Tyseley, usually consisting of three round trips per day and featuring a variety of their locomotives, as well as many visiting steam engines from all the companies. In addition to these trips, there have been many special charters to Stratford-on-Avon, notably in the 1980s from Marylebone, which joined the North Warwickshire Line at Bearley Junction. Other specials have used the whole length of the line, particularly from the north and east of England, via Saltley and Bordesley Junction.

The following is a small selection of 'specials' that have been seen on the line over the years.

Above On 19 December 1999 ex-GWR 'Hall' Class 4-6-0 No 4965 *Rood Ashton Hall* (newly restored by Tyseley) leaves the Stratford upon Avon line at Tyseley Junction and heads for Birmingham Snow Hill station with 'The Shakespeare Express'. These trains, run by Tyseley Museum, are now a regular feature on the Stratford line. *RS*

Above right On 7 June 1986, 'Castle' Class 4-6-0 No 7029 *Clun Castle* climbs the 1 in 150 through Danzey station with a Stratford-Birmingham train. *RS*

Right One of the earlier steam specials on the line was on 26 October 1974, when ex-SR 'Merchant Navy' 'Pacific' No 35028 *Clan Line* hauled a return special from Didcot to Stratford-on-Avon. It is seen climbing the 1 in 75 of Wilmcote bank on the return working from Stratford. *RS*

When the world-record-breaking steam locomotive ex-LNER 'A4' 'Pacific' No 4468 *Mallard* made a return to steam in 1986, it ran a special from London Marylebone to Stratford-on-Avon on Sunday 2 November. The immaculate-looking 'Pacific' is seen leaving Stratford on the return journey to Marylebone. Note the superb Pullman coaches and also the small plaque on the front of the locomotive, to denote that it is the holder of the world speed record for a steam engine of 126 mph, which was achieved in 1938. *RS*

On 8 May 1998 ex-GWR 'King' Class 4-6-0 No 6024 *King Edward I* and support coach run through Birmingham Snow Hill station on their way to Bristol (via Stourbridge Junction and Worcester Shrub Hill) in order to take out a special charter to Plymouth and Par the following day. *RS*

'Jubilee' Class 4-6-0 *Kholapur* is seen at speed between Wood End and The Lakes stations with a Stratford-Birmingham special on 7 June 1986. *RS*

Another of Tyseley's fine fleet of steam locomotives, 'Castle' Class 4-6-0 No 5080 *Defiant*, is seen just south of Wood End Tunnel on 15 April 1990 with the 1550 Tyseley to Stratford train. *RS*

STRATFORD TO CHELTENHAM

Stratford-on-Avon

This view of Stratford-on-Avon shed, looking north, was taken in 1960, and shows BR Standard Class '9F' 2-10-0 No 92229 at the coaling ramp. The shed normally stabled two or three 2-6-2 tanks overnight, plus a couple of ex-GWR Collett Class '3MT' 0-6-0s. It was a sub-shed of Tyseley, closed in September 1962.

In today's view, taken on 6 February 1997, there is nothing whatever to tell us that there was a locomotive shed on this site. As can be seen, the whole area is now an industrial estate. *PAB Publications/RS*

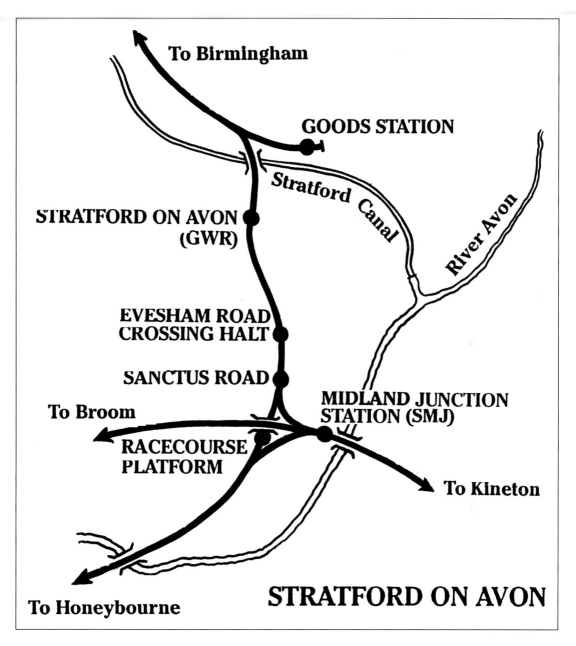

To Birmingham

GOODS STATION

Stratford Canal

River Avon

STRATFORD ON AVON
(GWR)

EVESHAM ROAD
CROSSING HALT

SANCTUS ROAD

MIDLAND JUNCTION
STATION (SMJ)

To Broom

RACECOURSE
PLATFORM

To Kineton

To Honeybourne

STRATFORD ON AVON

On 23 May 1959 ex-GWR Class '3MT' 0-6-0 No 2257 banks the main portion of the 'Cornishman' out of Stratford station, the train's engine being 'Castle' Class 4-6-0 No 5070 *Sir Daniel Gooch*. On the left a DMU awaits its turn of duty, and on the right, below the high warehouse, can be seen the locomotive shed building.

There are many similarities in today's scene, taken on 6 February 1997, as we see the rear of Class 150 unit No 150017 departing from Stratford with the 1527 to Stourbridge Junction. There is still semaphore signalling, albeit of the upper-quadrant variety, and the main trackwork is still in place, but the sidings and locomotive shed are no more; the warehouse and tall chimney have gone, but the gas-holder survives. New lighting has replaced the old lamps. *Michael Mensing/RS*

G.W.R.

STRATFORD-ON-AVON

The first railway reached Stratford in 1859 from Honeybourne, this being part of the Oxford, Worcester & Wolverhampton Railway (OW&WR), and the first station was at Sancta Lane, as it was originally called. This station was closed in 1863, and a temporary facility was opened by the Alcester road. This remained in use until the present station was opened in 1865, once again beside the Alcester road. It originally had an overall roof, but this disappeared at the beginning of the century, when expansion of the station took place.

In the late 1950s ex-GWR '3F' 0-6-0 pannier tank No 9429 prepares to leave Stratford with a southbound local train. In the same place on 6 February 1997 Class 150 unit No 150017 has just arrived at Stratford with the 1358 from Stourbridge Junction, which will later form the 1527 return working. The attractive-looking building on the right-hand side has now gone, as has some of the trackwork on the left, but all the other buildings seem to be there, with the addition of flower beds and new lighting to replace the old. Stratford is now the terminus of the line, the through route to Cheltenham having closed in 1976. *Lens of Sutton/RS*

A few hundred yards south of Stratford station the line crossed over the main Evesham road (A439), necessitating a level crossing and a signal box to control it. In March 1960 it was possible to see two boxes at this location. The original dated from 1891 and is in stark contrast with its replacement, built in 1960; the new box came into use on 12 June of that year.

There is little in today's picture, taken on 6 February 1997, to compare with the previous one except for the house, the chimneys of which can be seen above the two signal boxes. The trackbed is now a new road, and the photograph was taken from a traffic island that is part of the Evesham road. *PAB Publications/RS*

This view of an unidentified GWR 2-6-0 approaching Sanctus Lane bridge with a northbound goods was taken around 1935. At this point there was a connection with the Stratford-upon-Avon & Midland Junction Railway (SMJ), which crossed over the Honeybourne line a few hundred yards south of this location (see the map on page 67). The SMJ ran from Ravenstone Wood Junction, on the Midland line to Northampton, to Broom, south of Alcester on the Redditch to Ashchurch line. The SMJ station in Stratford closed in 1952, and the line closed in 1965. All that is left now is a 4-mile section from Fenny Compton to the MOD depot at Kineton. The 'present' picture was taken on 6 February 1997, and it is very hard to tell that a railway once existed at this location. *PAB Publications/RS*

When this photograph of Stratford Racecourse Platform (looking south) was taken in the 1950s, the connection with the SMJ, which would come in from the left of the picture and meet the GWR line immediately south of the station, had not yet been constructed. This south curve was put in place in 1958 and opened in 1960, with the closure of the Stratford-Broom line to freight traffic. This connection, together with the new one put in at Fenny Compton in 1960, allowed heavy freight traffic to travel to and from the South Midlands and South Wales via the GWR route. The Racecourse station was opened in 1933, but in BR days, apart from major race days, was under-used.

Today's view of the same location, taken on 20 February 1997, shows the trackbed now used as a cycle track and walkway, known as the 'Greenway.' Only the hedgerows and background hills identify the location.

Before leaving the Stratford area, it should be noted that there were also two small halts - Evesham Road Crossing Halt, north of the Racecourse station, and Chambers Crossing Halt, south of Racecourse. Opened in 1904, they had short lives, both closing in 1916. *Lens of Sutton/RS*

Milcote and Long Marston

After crossing over the River Avon (just under a mile from the Racecourse station), the next station on the line was at Milcote, some 3 miles from Stratford. From the nameboard it will be seen that the station also served the nearby villages of Weston and Welford. This view of Milcote station, taken in the early 1960s, is looking towards Honeybourne and also shows the single platform of the original station, which opened in 1859. The line was doubled in 1907/8 when the new station was opened.

The present-day picture, taken on 14 February 1997, shows part of the northbound platform still in place and the trackbed that forms the 'Greenway' cycle track/walkway. *Lens of Sutton/RS*

Opposite page Like Milcote, Long Marston opened in 1859 and closed to passenger traffic in 1966. This general view of the station, looking towards Stratford, was taken on 27 November 1965. Because of the single-line level crossing the original northbound platform was situated behind the photographer on a loop line, but with the doubling of the line in 1907/8 it was rebuilt opposite the southbound platform.

On 14 February 1997 it can be seen that most of the area is now a factory site. Possibly the trees on the extreme left are the same in both pictures. *Norman Preedy/RS*

Long Marston is the headquarters of the recently formed Stratford-on-Avon & Broadway Railway Society, whose basic aim is one day to reach Stratford to the north and Honeybourne and Broadway to the south. This view of the MOD yard at Long Marston, looking towards Stratford, was taken on 15 February 1997, and clearly shows the old trackbed of the main line on the left, leading to the factory building seen in the 'present' picture opposite. The line coming in from the bottom of the picture is from Honeybourne, some 2 or 3 miles to the south.

When the line closed in 1976 this section was retained to service the MOD yard and scrapyard at Long Marston. This picture gives some idea of the size of the MOD depot (which is scheduled for closure in 1999) and also shows some of the stock of the newly formed railway society. *RS*

There were two halts between Long Marston and Honeybourne: Broad Marston, which closed in 1916, and Pebworth Halt, closed in 1966. On Sunday 18 May 1958 ex-GWR 'Castle' Class 4-6-0 No 5007 *Rougemont Castle* hurries past Pebworth Halt with an 'Amateur Photographer' special from Paddington (9.15 am) to Stratford-on-Avon. The same location on 14 February 1997 shows what is now the single-track branch from Honeybourne to Long Marston. *Michael Mensing/RS*

Honeybourne and Broadway

ack
June 2/06

GREAT WESTERN RAILWAY.

Circular No. $\frac{F. 1654.}{R. 1283.}$

PADDINGTON STATION,
28th MAY, 1906.

Cheltenham and Honeybourne Line.

With reference to Circular No. $\frac{F. 1556}{R. 1263}$ dated January 25th, 1905, the Cheltenham and Honeybourne New Line is now completed as far as Bishop's Cleeve, and on **Friday, June 1st, 1906, Cretton Halt (to pick up and set down Passengers only), Gotherington and Bishop's Cleeve Stations** will be opened for traffic. It is expected that the remaining portion of the New Line will be opened through to Cheltenham on August 1st.

PASSENGER AND PARCELS TRAFFIC.

The Service for Passenger and Parcels Traffic on the New Line will be worked by Rail Motor Service (one class only), and 1st, 2nd and 3rd class Fares between Gotherington and Bishop's Cleeve Stations on the New Line, and Stations beyond Honeybourne, will be put into operation, enabling Passengers to travel by Rail Motor on the New Line and 1st, 2nd or 3rd class by Ordinary Train to and from Honeybourne.

Through Fares and Rates will be supplied as required.

Parcels may be booked through to and from your Station and Gotherington and Bishop's Cleeve Stations at the Clearing House scale.

Insert in alphabetical order Gotherington and Bishop's Cleeve Stations on your Local Stations Card.

GOODS TRAFFIC.

Extensive lists of Rates are being issued with Gotherington and Bishop's Cleeve, but if any beyond those provided are required, application must be made to your District Goods Manager.

The Company will not for the present undertake cartage at these places, and Rates must not be quoted as including this service.

A GWR circular from May 1906 giving details of progress on the building of the Cheltenham and Honeybourne line.

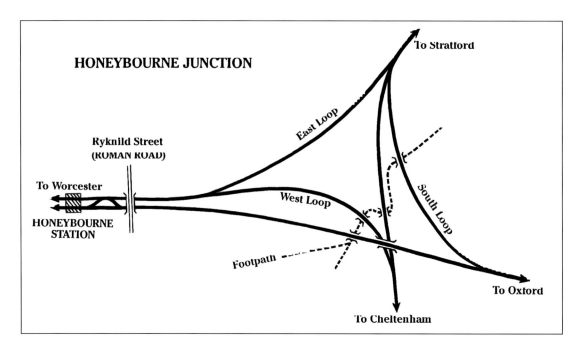

HONEYBOURNE JUNCTION

Ryknild Street
(ROMAN ROAD)

To Worcester

HONEYBOURNE
STATION

East Loop

West Loop

South Loop

Footpath

To Stratford

To Oxford

To Cheltenham

On 14 August 1965 ex-LMS Class '5' 4-6-0 No 45006 approaches Honeybourne Junction from the south with the 12.30 pm Penzance-Wolverhampton (Low Level) train. Just behind the photographer is the Worcester to Oxford line, which crosses over the Cheltenham line at this point. The line swinging away to the right is the West Loop (see the map opposite), which, after passing beneath the Worcester-Oxford line, joined up with the East Loop from the Stratford line, now part of the branch to Long Marston, then entered Honeybourne station about a mile to the west of this location.

The 'present' view, taken on 14 February 1997, shows that the trackbed is still there, and also the same road bridge and houses.

Honeybourne station was closed to passengers in 1969 and by 1971 the Worcester-Oxford line was mainly single track. However, Honeybourne was re-opened as a halt in 1981 (using the old down main line platform), partly as a result of the opening of Long Lartin Prison and with pressure from the Cotswold Line Promotion Group. *Michael Mensing/RS*

G.W.R.

Honeybourne

G.W.R.

Bretforton
AND
Weston-sub-Edge

This page The next station south of Honeybourne Junction was Weston-sub-Edge, which opened in 1904 and closed to passenger traffic in 1960. This view, looking north, dates from around 1960, while the 'present' equivalent was taken on 14 February 1997, and shows that all that now remains to remind us that there once was a railway line here is the trackbed. *Lens of Sutton/RS*

Opposite page Situated roughly equidistant between Weston-sub-Edge and Broadway is the Cotswold village of Willersey, and this picture, taken in the late 1950s and looking north, shows the halt that served the village. It opened in 1904 and was closed in 1960, and featured a typical GWR 'pagoda'-style waiting room. On 4 February 1997 nothing except part of the trackbed, which is now a walkway, survives. *Lens of Sutton/RS*

Since leaving Stratford the line has run through the county of Warwick, but the next location - the famous Cotswold town of Broadway - is situated in the eastern edge of Worcestershire. On 4 August 1950 'Castle' Class 4-6-0 No 5015 *Kingswear Castle* makes a fine sight as it approaches Broadway station with a southbound express. On the right is the horse dock and siding. The same location is seen on 28 December 1996, the trackbed, cutting and distant bridge identifying the location. *PAB Publications/RS*

G. W. R.

BROADWAY
(WORCESTER)

This photograph of Broadway station was taken around 1958, and shows a Cheltenham-Honeybourne local train about to depart on its northbound journey. Opened in 1904 and closed in 1960, the station boasted a small goods yard and goods shed at the southern end of the site, which remained open until 1964.

In its heyday Broadway was a reasonably busy station, with a fair amount of freight traffic being generated locally; apart from the Station Master's accommodation, houses were also provided for some of the staff. These were situated at the top of the main drive, which was adjacent to the station on the eastern side, the drive coming off the Evesham road (A44) over which the line crossed at the southern end of the station. *R. S. Carpenter collection/RS*

The Gloucestershire Warwickshire Railway: Toddington, Winchcombe and Gotherington

Two miles south of Broadway was Laverton Halt, which opened in 1905 and closed in 1960. On 1 March 1964 ex-GWR 'Grange' Class 4-6-0 No 6846 *Ruckley Grange* is seen about a mile south of the halt, with a northbound (Sunday) engineering train. The location is where the line passed under the A46 (now the B4632) Cheltenham to Broadway road.

The same scene on 14 February 1997 shows the trackbed and occupation bridge in the distance still in place. This is now part of the Gloucester Warwickshire Railway, which hopes to extend to Broadway and perhaps to Stratford in the not too distant future. *Michael Mensing/RS*

A mile or so south of the previous picture, after crossing Stanway viaduct, we come to Toddington, which is the operational headquarters of the Gloucestershire Warwickshire Railway. This picture of the station was taken in the early 1960s, looking south towards Hayles Abbey Halt. Has anything changed in the 'present' view, taken on Boxing Day 1996? Not a great deal, but now everything is in much better order, with the addition of more seating and more lights on the station. Also note the water tower.

Toddington station was opened in 1904, closed to passenger traffic in 1960, and to goods traffic in 1967. Over the years the location became derelict, losing its platforms, but happily after the closure of the line in 1976 the preservation society was formed and by 1981 it had purchased the trackbed and then set about renovating the station, the results of which we can see in the 'present' picture. Since this picture was taken a new four-road locomotive shed has been built, out of sight on the right beyond the station. Among the locomotives to be accommodated there will be the line's newly acquired diesels, two Class 37s, a Class 24 and a Class 20, while being restored are a 'Peak' and a Class 26. *Lens of Sutton/RS*

Another view of Toddington station, this time from the southbound platform. The date is 27 February 1960, and ex-GWR 0-6-0 pannier tank No 9727 pauses at the station with the 1.00 pm Cheltenham to Broadway train.

On 26 December 1996 the rear of the 2.00 pm to Gretton is seen in the distance as it leaves Toddington. The train engine is ex-GWR 'Modified Hall' Class 4-6-0 No 6960 *Raveningham Hall*. The left-hand canopy looks different, but most other things look nearly the same, a tribute to the efforts of the Gloucestershire Warwickshire Railway. 1n the middle distance can be seen the goods yard (and shed) where stock is stabled and locomotive maintenance work is carried out. *Hugh Ballantyne/RS*

Gt. Western Ry.   Gt. Western Ry.
Toddington   Toddington
              TO
       PADDINGTON
       Via Oxford & Reading
  Rail Motor Car to Honeybourne and
  First Class beyond
  Fare 16/8
  Paddington   Paddington
                          back F, N

The final pictures at Toddington station are looking towards Stratford. The 'past' scene, also taken on 27 February 1960, shows a cross-country DMU in original green livery speeding through the station with the 12.25 pm from Birmingham Snow Hill to Carmarthen.

On 26 December 1996 the empty stock of the 1.00 pm train to Gretton waits for its locomotive (No 6960). It is hoped that by the time this book goes to press trains will be running as far as Gotherington, some 6 miles from Toddington, and by the turn of the century to Cheltenham Racecourse station.

Before leaving Toddington, mention must be made of the splendid station bookshop, and the excellent 'Flag and Whistle' cafeteria to the west side of the station. The author can vouch for the scrumptious home-made cakes! *Hugh Ballantyne/RS*

Ex-GWR '1400' Class 0-4-2 tank No 1424 restarts the 1.17 pm Honeybourne to Cheltenham train from Hayles Abbey Halt on 27 February 1960; the halt was opened in 1928 and closed in 1960. The auto-trailer is W2338W.

The halt has now completely gone and only the background fields and shape of the embankments identify with the earlier picture. On 28 December 1996 the train is the 2.00 pm from Toddington hauled by No 6960. *Hugh Ballantyne/RS*

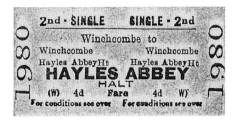

Between 1998 and 2002 BR Standard Class '9F' 2-10-0 No 92203 (formerly *Black Prince*), owned by the renowned artist David Shepherd, worked on the Gloucestershire Warwickshire Railway, and is seen here climbing out of Winchcombe with the 13.20 from Toddington. *RS*

Opposite page Leaving Broadway the line now runs through Gloucestershire, and our next location is Winchcombe, where this picture of the station, looking towards Toddington, was taken in 1960, the year of its closure (it had opened in 1905).

When the Gloucestershire Warwickshire Railway took over the line in the late 1970s, there was nothing left of the station, so what you see in the 'present' picture, taken on 26 December 1996, has all been rebuilt from scratch - a remarkable achievement. The station building is from Monmouth Troy, the signal box is from Birmingham Hall Green, and its lever frame from Honeybourne West Loop. Also, the Carriage & Wagon Maintenance Depot of the preserved line is situated in the goods yard at Winchcombe. *G. Tilt, PAB Publications/RS*

Opposite page Two views of Winchcombe station, almost complete, taken on 8 March 2003. The first shows the new station footbridge in place and the other, looking in the opposite direction, shows the yard and the Carriage & Wagon works. *Both RS*

Right A GWR circular relating to the opening of Winchcombe station in 1905 'for all descriptions of traffic'.

Private and not for Publication.

GREAT WESTERN RAILWAY.

Circular No. F. 1556.
R. 1262.

PADDINGTON STATION,
JANUARY 25TH, 1905.

OPENING OF WINCHCOMBE STATION

(CHELTENHAM AND HONEYBOURNE LINE).

With reference to Circular No. F. 1540, dated November 28th, 1904, the R. 1256, Cheltenham and Honeybourne new Line is now completed as far as Winchcombe, and on **Wednesday, February 1st, 1905, Winchcombe Station will be opened for all descriptions of traffic.**

PASSENGER AND PARCELS TRAFFIC.

The Service for Passenger and Parcels Traffic on the new Line will be worked by Rail Motor Service (one class only), and 1st, 2nd and 3rd class Fares between Winchcombe on the new Line, and Stations beyond Honeybourne, will be put into operation, enabling Passengers to travel by Rail Motor and 1st, 2nd or 3rd class by Ordinary Train to and from Honeybourne.

The Rail Motor will also run several trips daily from Honeybourne to Evesham, and Honeybourne to Stratford-on-Avon.

Through Fares and Rates will be supplied as required.

Parcels may be booked through to and from your Station and **Winchcombe** at the Clearing House scale.

Insert Winchcombe in alphabetical order on your Local Stations Card.

GOODS TRAFFIC.

An extensive list of Rates has been issued, but if any, beyond those provided, are required please make application for them to your District Goods Manager.

The undermentioned accommodation is provided :—

Goods Shed, Carriage Sheets, Horse Landing, Cart Weighbridge and Cattle Pens.

There is also a Cartage Establishment and the Company will undertake the collection and delivery of ordinary traffic at Winchcombe.

Below The winter sunshine glows off *Raveningham Hall* as it climbs out of Winchcombe and heads towards Greet Tunnel with the 12 noon service from Toddington on 28 December 1996. *RS*

Turning to look in the opposite direction from the previous picture, and over 30 years earlier, 'Britannia' 'Pacific' No 70045 (formerly *Lord Rowallan*) is seen leaving the 693-yard-long Greet Tunnel with the 11.10 am Ilfracombe-Wolverhampton (Low Level) summer Saturday train. The date is 26 June 1965. Today's picture, taken on 28 December 1996, shows No 6960 returning from just west of Gretton Halt with the 11.00 am round trip from Toddington. The line is now only single track, and the lineside hut has gone, but a new semaphore signal is in place, and of course most of all steam trains once again run on this line - remember that only the trackbed was left after 1976. *Michael Mensing/RS*

On 14 August 1965 Brush Type 4 No D1590 is caught by the camera between Gotherington and Gretton Halt, again with the 11.10 Ilfracombe-Wolverhampton (Low Level) train. The motive power for this train varied between steam and diesel at this period. The small halt at Gretton opened in 1906 and closed in 1960. At the time of writing Gloucestershire Warwickshire Railway trains run to Far Stanley, just west of Gretton.

In this 'present' view, dated 28 December 1996, it can be seen that the track has been relaid in readiness for the running of trains to Gotherington. *Michael Mensing/RS*

This picture of Gotherington station (opened in 1906 and closed in 1955), looking east, was taken in 1966 and gives a good idea of the state of dereliction that it was in at that time. Fortunately the station was bought by Mr Bryan Nicholls, who kindly gave the author permission to take the 'present' picture. Following the purchase Mr Nicholls set about restoring the station to its former glory (including the station platform, which had also gone) and the splendid results can be seen in the 'present' picture, taken on 28 December 1996. Mr Nicholls also built the southbound platform for the preserved line, using the edging stones from Withington on the old Midland & South Western Junction (MSWJ) line. Trains began calling at Gotherington from the summer of 2003, but for walkers only, as the station has no vehicular access and there is no car park. *Lens of Sutton/RS*

Cheltenham

The station at Bishops Cleeve, some 4 miles north of Cheltenham, was opened in 1906 and closed along with many others on the line in 1960. This view, taken in the early 1960s, is looking towards Cheltenham and shows the edge of the small goods yard (opposite the signal box), which remained open until 1963. The motor scooter on the platform is also worthy of note! On 15 February 1997 all that remained was the trackbed. *Lens of Sutton/RS*

Among many things, Cheltenham has always been famous for its racecourse, which is located on the north-eastern outskirts of this Regency town. In 1912 the Great Western Railway opened a station by the racecourse; this remained open until 1968, although it opened occasionally in the 1970s, mainly for race meetings, the last time being in March 1976. On 29 March 1975 'Western' Class 52 diesel-hydraulic No D1052 *Western Viceroy* pauses at the station with a Plymouth Railway Circle special train to Stratford and Birmingham.

The second view of the racecourse station was taken on 15 February 1997 before the track was relaid and the station re-

opened by the Gloucestershire Warwickshire Railway. On the left-hand side of the picture, behind the tree, is the old station booking office, which at that time was being maintained by the famous Cheltenham building firm of Westbury's. *Norman Preedy/RS*

Just south of Cheltenham Racecourse station is the short Hunting Butts Tunnel. On 26 June 1965 Brush Type 4 No D1588 is about to enter the tunnel's southern portal with the 2.30 pm Penzance-Wolverhampton (Low Level) train. By 15 February 1997 the trackbed has become a walkway, but recently the tunnel has been closed. The walkway starts just south of the site of Cheltenham Malvern Road station. *Michael Mensing/RS*

This historic picture of High Street Halt, Cheltenham, is undated, but must have been taken between 1908 and 1917, the opening and closing dates of the halt. The train approaching is a steam railmotor service from Honeybourne. Today only the trackbed (now a walkway) and the bridge girders over the High Street are a reminder of the 'past' picture. *Lens of Sutton/RS*

Between High Street Halt and Cheltenham Malvern Road station was the junction for the short spur to Cheltenham St James station. This was situated to the east of the line almost in the centre of the town and was built in 1847 as the terminus for Gloucester and London trains, and known as Cheltenham Station. It became Cheltenham St James in 1908, and in 1923 the GWR inaugurated the 'Cheltenham Flyer' from this station. It was also the terminus station for trains from the Midland & South West Junction line from Swindon and Andover, as well as the services from Kingham. Both these services were withdrawn in the early 1960s, and the station itself closed in 1966. This late 1950s view of St James shows well the grand exterior of the station. On 9 February 1997 the site is occupied by the offices of Mercantile & General Re-Insurance, but the Regency houses on the right-hand side are still there. *Lens of Sutton/RS*

Ex-GWR 2-6-0 No 5306 is pictured coming off the turntable at Cheltenham St James after working in with an RCTS railtour over the MSWJ railways on 10 September 1961. The station platforms can be seen on the right hand side. At the site of the station on 9 February 1997 only the Church of St Gregory the Great survives to identify with the 'past' picture. *Norman Preedy/RS*

Back on the Cheltenham-Stratford line, 'Castle' Class 4-6-0 No 7026 *Tenby Castle* enters Cheltenham Malvern Road station in March 1961 with train X07, a Cheltenham Gold Cup return race special to Paddington. The train is on the station avoiding line. The bridge in the background carries Malvern Road over the line, and just beyond that was the junction for St James station.

Today this area is a builder's yard, but the background houses are still there, as is the road bridge, which now passes over the walkway that is off the right-hand side of the picture. *Norman Preedy/RS*

Malvern Road station was opened in 1908 and closed, with St James, in 1966. It consisted of one island platform, reached by a footbridge from the booking office situated on the down side of the station. There was also a short bay platform (177 feet long) cut into the eastern end of the down platform, as seen on the right of the previous 'past' picture). On 26 August 1961 ex-GWR '51XX' Class 2-6-2 tank No 5182 leaves Malvern Road with a Kingham-Cheltenham St James local train. The start of the bay platform can be seen on the left, and in the background is the locomotive shed and goods yard. On 9 February 1997 only the trackbed and the edge of the cutting remain to remind us of the past. *R. S. Carpenter collection/RS*

This view of Malvern Road shed (showing the Second World War extension) was taken in the 1950s and shows ex-GWR 0-6-0 pannier tank No 5418 and ex-GWR 2-6-0s Nos 4358 and 6381. All the locomotives carry the shed code 85B, Gloucester (Horton Road), of which Malvern Road was a sub-shed. The depot closed in 1964, and the site is now occupied by a builder's warehouse, as seen on 15 February 1997. *R. S. Carpenter collection/RS*

At Malvern Road station on 2 July 1960 ex-SR Class 'U' 2-6-0 No 3I791 pauses with a Southampton to Cheltenham St James train (via the MSWJ line). This view also shows the coaling stage and part of the goods yard. Except for the trees, nothing remains on 14 February 1997 to remind us that this was once a busy station and goods yard. *Norman Preedy/RS*

Ex-GWR 'Hall' Class 4-6-0 No 5951 *Clyffe Hall* approaches Cheltenham Spa Malvern Road West Signal Box on 24 August 1948 with a northbound goods train. Almost 50 years later, on 9 February 1997, this location is now the start of a walkway/cycle track. Note the road bridge, which can be seen in the earlier picture, and also the children's play locomotive, a somewhat poignant reminder of the 'past' picture. *PAB Publications/RS*

Our journey's end is at Lansdown Junction, looking north in the summer of 1967, with the Midland line coming from Lansdown station on the left and the GWR route from Malvern Road on the right. Completing the scene is Type 4 No D127 in charge of a southbound passenger train. At the old Lansdown Junction on 15 February 1997 Class 47 No 47822 pulls out of the surviving Midland station with a Liverpool-Plymouth train (1142 ex-Cheltenham). A small warehouse now straddles most of the GWR line, a colour light signal has replaced the gantry, and the telegraph lines have gone. *G. Tilt, PAB Publications/RS*

INDEX OF LOCATIONS

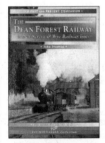